SMIKE

From the BBC television production of Smike

Exclusive distributors:
Music Sales Limited
78 Newman Street
London W1P 3LA
Music Sales PTY Limited
27 Clarendon Street
Artarmon, Sydney
Australia 2064.

SMIKE

CONTENTS

Act 1

Act 2

SMIKE

A POP MUSICAL FREELY BASED ON CHARLES DICKENS' NICHOLAS NICKLEBY.

WRITTEN BY ROGER HOLMAN & SIMON MAY.

BASED ON AN ORIGINAL PRODUCTION BY THE BOYS OF KINGSTON GRAMMAR SCHOOL (LIBRETTO WRITTEN BY ROGER HOLMAN, SIMON MAY AND CLIVE BARNETT).

PREFACE

Since the first performance of SMIKE in 1973, SMIKE has been adapted for BBC Television by Paul Ciani and John Morley, revised and added to for different versions in the U.K., South Africa and Eire, by Peter Coe (director of the original production of OLIVER), Pinetown Junior School (Durban), Ken Linge, Bill Cadman, the boys of Christian Brothers, Synge Street (Dublin) and Holmewood House School (Tunbridge Wells). These are only some of those who have involved themselves with SMIKE, and to all those others not mentioned please accept our apologies.

It has been interesting to see that every production has been completely different, and so even now the present libretto is by no means definitive. The songs and libretto are now available for any school or amateur dramatic society to use to meet the requirements of their own production. Many variations are possible. For example the inclusion of girls in both the 19th and 20th Century sequences is possible. Some schools may wish to exclude the Saracens Head Scene (Act 1 scene 2) and go straight from the 20th Century classroom to Dotheboys Hall. Not all the scene changes may be possible, and for the Dotheboys Hall scenes an ingenious designer may well decide to incorporate the Squeers parlour room and the boys' quarters into one composite set. It is our view that the only requirement for a successful production of SMIKE is an open mind, a sense of fun, a love of Dickens and music, and plenty of energy!

The libretto to SMIKE is available from Music Sales Ltd., 78, Newman Street, London W.1.

An LP of the BBC TV version of SMIKE is available on Pye Records (NSPL 18423) We would be grateful if producers would include this information on their programme notes!

All rights of performance of this work are reserved. Permission to perform SMIKE can be obtained by writing to ATV Music Ltd., 26-27 Regency Square, Brighton BN1 2FH

Act One

Overture (Going To School) Dawn Music

Words and music by Roger Holman and Simon May

2

6

Ab C⁷sus4 C7 Fm

Tom-toms

Daily Test Chant

Elaborate and regimented musical ritual in unison.
The class bring out pens and paper, and their comments
on the Test are counterposed to the questions asked by the Headmaster.

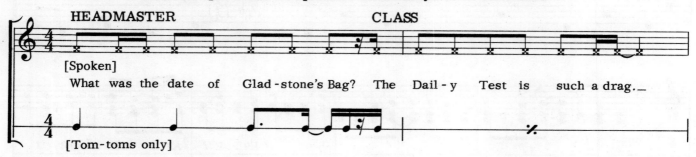

HEADMASTER   CLASS

[Spoken]
What was the date of Glad-stone's Bag? The Dail-y Test is such a drag.

[Tom-toms only]

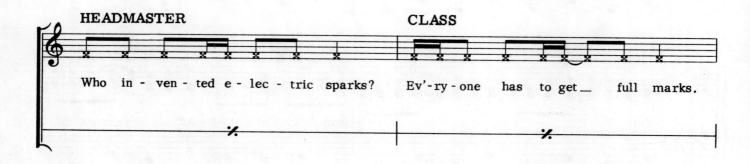

HEADMASTER   CLASS

Who in-ven-ted e-lec-tric sparks? Ev'-ry-one has to get full marks.

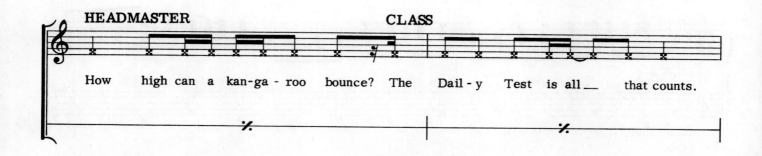

HEADMASTER   CLASS

How high can a kan-ga-roo bounce? The Dail-y Test is all that counts.

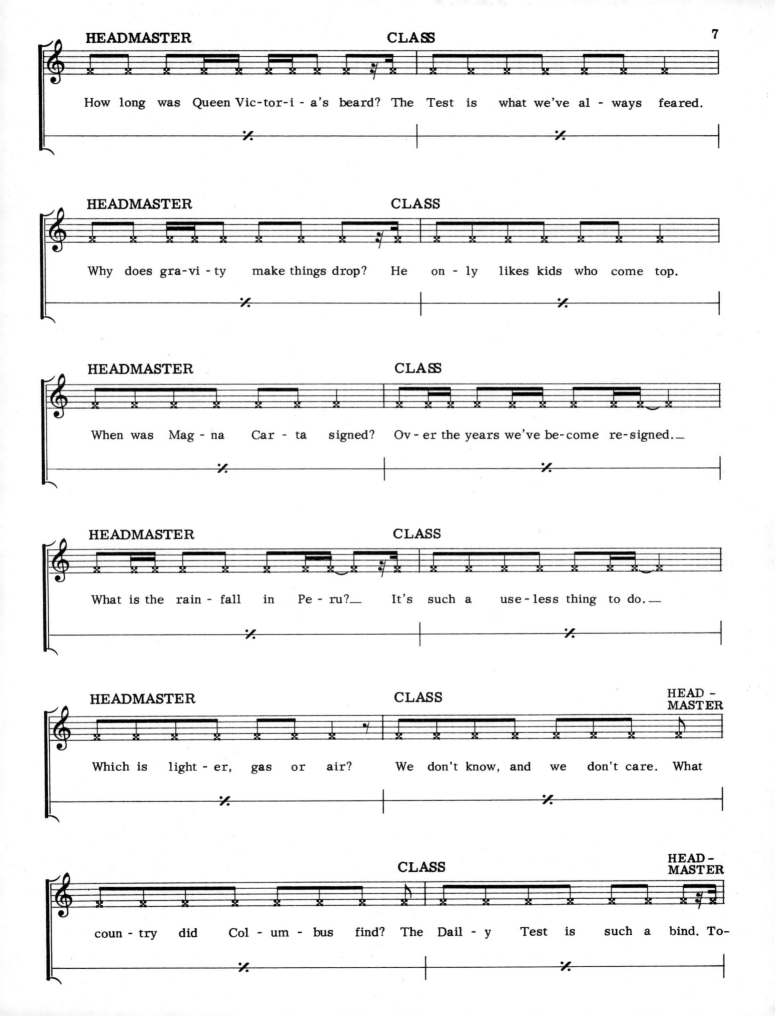

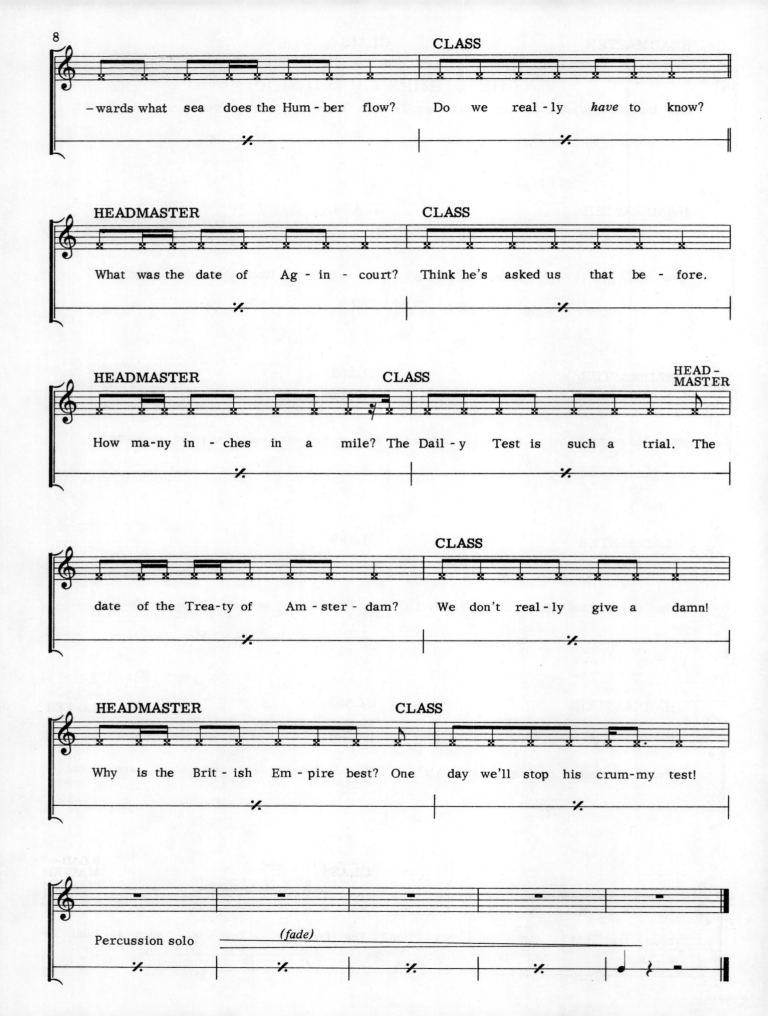

Doing Things By Numbers

Fairly bright tempo (Reggae feel) ♩ = 112

12

Here I Am

cue ——

COATES: Who wants to read about another school?
This one's bad enough.

BROWN: Why should we listen to you, anyway?
PLANK: No one ever listens to us.
MARSH: Yeah. If you've got summink to say,
you should be allowed to say it.

PLANK: Yeah. That's freedom of speech.
NICHOLLS: Then why don't you listen to me?

Stop! And Just Think Who You Could Be

cue _____

HEADMASTER: No, you're quite right. I'm not entirely convinced,
Mr Nicholls, but your idea might just be feasible.

(children cheer excitedly)

Optional 3rd verse for production with mixed cast (4 bars to ✱)

GIRLS

[Spoken]
It's all about a boys' school.

C   B♭ add 9   C   B♭ add 9

BOYS   GIRLS   BOYS   ✱

So what! So what a-bout the girls then?   Hold on, we'll think of some thing for you.

C   B♭ add 9   C   B♭ add 9   C

Dance routine

Drums only

(ad lib.)

CHORUS

Stop! and just think__ who you could be!   Stop! and just think__ who you could be!

C   B♭ add 9   C   B♭ add 9

Transition Music

We've Got The Youngsters' Interests At Heart

cue _____

SQUEERS: He goes along down with me tomorrow.
That's his luggage that he's a-sittin' upon now.
Not a very big parcel you may be thinking, but
where's the sense in bringing lots of clothes
when he's only going to grow out of 'em?

(BOYS huddle around the BOY on the settle)

SNAWLEY: The victuals at this Hall of yours, Mr Squeers,
must be very advantageous to a young boy's growth.

SQUEERS: Oh indeed, they are. Indeed they are.

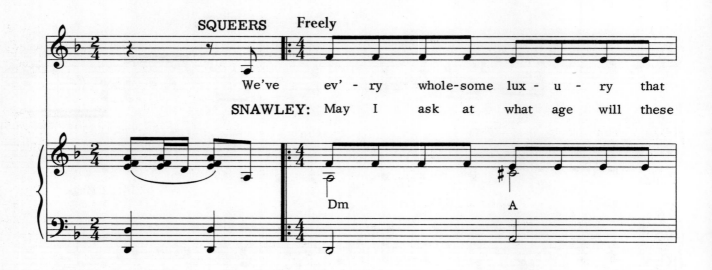

30

Wackford, Fanny, Squeersy and Me

cue _____

SQUEERS: (indicating Mrs Squeers, Fanny and Wackford)
Well, Nickleby, there's a picture for you.
What d'you think of them?

NICHOLAS: Very fine, Sir.

SQUEERS: You won't see such a family as this very often I think.
I should like to know how I should ever get on without them.

boys,— Sir,   The   pride of   Dothe - boys   Hall.___
tron-o-my   With   all   the   things__ he's   fed, ___   The

D6   Dma7   Em7   A11   A

That wo-man nev-er   chan - ges,   She means so much__ to me.__
i - dol of his mum and   pa - pa,   A   bless- ing to ____ us all.__

G   A/G   F#m7   Bm7   Em7   A

___   The   ve - ry   first   time we   met,— I   loved _   that
___   There's flesh on him for twen-ty   boys, — Sir. _____   You

D   D7   G   A/G   F#m7   Bm7

CHORUS

bu - st - ling, live - ly   crea-ture you   see. _____   Oh,   We're
couldn't find bet-ter   at   Doth-e - boys Hall. _____   Oh,

Em7   D/F#   G   A11   A

36

Dotheboys Hall

cue _____

SQUEERS: I do not know her equal, I just do not know her equal.
That woman, Nickleby, is always the same, – same
bustling, lively, active, saving creature that you see
her. A real mother to the boys, and what they lack in
material comforts we make up for in love and charity.

(cue INTRO. for song: 'DOTHEBOYS HALL')

Love and charity, Mr Nickleby, love and charity.

(He has come down the steps to join Mrs SQUEERS)

40

clothe, board, book, wash the sons of no-bil - i - ty
guide, mind, learn, love their ve - ry own fam - i - ly } At

Dothe-boys Hall, near Gre-ta Bridge we live in har - mo - ny.

ny.

Doing Things By Numbers (Reprise)

cue ____

SQUEERS: When I say number one, the first boy in each line
may take a drink; and when I say number two, the
next boy may, and so on until the last boy.
Are you ready?

(Instrumental verse as milk is passed around.
SQUEERS sings, "One, two, three, four, five"
as each BOY comes to his turn. BOYS move away
from Mr and Mrs Squeers after receiving their milk.)

Better Off The Way I Am

cue _____

SQUEERS: .....Good night then Nickleby, six o'clock in the morning mind,
and I'll show you myself where the pump is for you to wash.

(He exits Left with Mrs SQUEERS on his arm.

NICHOLAS looks around him and goes to the
carver chair and pulls it forward a little.
He stops and listens.

Lights dim on NICHOLAS and go up on SMIKE
who is huddled at the bottom of stairs Left.

SMIKE, unaware of NICHOLAS, sings-)

[1] Nev-er had a mum or dad __ to call my own, But it's

[2] Who can say I'm right or wrong __ to feel this way? I

fun-ny how you nev-er miss_____ the things___ you've nev-er known.___ Though
would-n't give the time of day to par - ents, an - y - way.___

Am7   Bb   C

some-thing in my life has gone___ that nev - er came,
No - thing you can do or say___ will change my mind.

Dm   Gm7

Ev'-ry-thing that I've lost___ has got to be___ my gain.___
Ev'-ry-thing I've seen of life___ is kill - ing me___ in - side.___

Am7   Bb   Gm7/C

CHORUS 3rd time saxophone solo for 4 bars.

[1-3] Par - ents, what kind of peo - ple do they think they are___ That
[2] Par - ents, what kind of peo - ple do they think they are? ___ It's

F   Gm

54

cue___

SMIKE: Who will talk to me in those long nights?
What faces will smile on me when I die?
You think you can help me, but you can't,
no one can. No one can find my father and mother. No hope...

(Cue INTRO. for song 'DON'T LET LIFE GET YOU DOWN')

...There's no hope.

NICHOLAS: Sssssssh. When I look at this wretched school I feel as unhappy as you,
but we must both say there's always hope.

Don't Let Life Get You Down

Act Two
Scene One
Dotheboys Hall – Classroom

cue: _____

The music starts while houselights are up.
Houselights dim slowly to BLACK.

Stage is set in darkness.
The classroom is now being used as a dormitory,
and BOYS are sleeping everywhere.
SMIKE is asleep Right.

Tabs open and a choir (BOYS) begins to hum.

Dawn Music

In The Warm Light Of A Brand New Day

SMIKE

To - day has come,__ I see the sun,__ It's shi-ning ev'-ry-where.__ A
(I) found a long lost hap-pi - ness__ When I woke up to-day;__ The

change of heart__ has just be-gun.__ The sil - ver li-ning's there,__ An' when I'm
cold I felt in - side of me __ Can now be pushed a - way, __ Cos when I'm

62

Dotheboys Rock

cue: _____

VOICE OFF: What's all this noise going on in 'ere?

(The BOYS scatter, terrified that it is Squeers.
A huge shadow of a person with a stick appears on the wall Left.
Below the stairs the BOYS cower in silence.
BOLDER enters at top of stairs mimicking SQUEERS.
He comes down amid general laughter.)

to coda

Do the boys rock,   Do — the boys   rock and   roll! —

Do the boys roll! yeh yeh! — Do the boys rock, Do—

— the boys rock and roll! — (spoken) Yeh!

5 Well, I'm thirty five and I'm still alive,
I got arthritis, but I still do the jive,
Oh yeh, reelin' and a-rockin'
Do the boys rock, Do the boys rock and roll.

6 Gonna pack my things and go hell-bound,
This heart-break hotel gets me down,
Wo yeh, reelin' and a-rockin'
Do the boys rock, Do the boys rock and roll.

[to Chorus]

Brimstone and Treacle

cue: _____

MRS SQUEERS: Fanny, the spoon.
FANNY: The spoon? Haven't you got it?
MRS SQUEERS: I thought you had it.
TOGETHER: Who's got the spoon?

(As the music begins MRS SQUEERS and FANNY search for the spoon.
In fact, one of the boys had it, and they now pass it along the line.
Their backs are turned to the Audience at this point and the spoon
can be seen changing from one hand to another.
Eventually MRS SQUEERS realizes what is going on. She pushes one boy
out of the line and, taking his place, grabs the spoon as it reaches her.)

Your Kind Of Woman

cue: _____

MRS SQUEERS: Come and sit down here with me. Have you ever had your fortune told?

(She picks up a pack of cards from the table.)

If you want to know the truth about your future, listen carefully and I will reveal all.

Freely

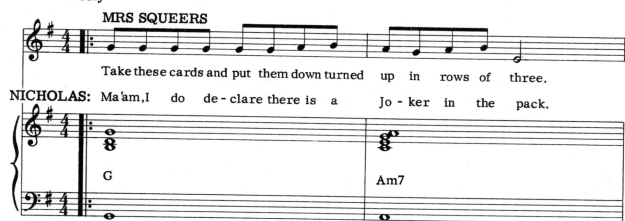

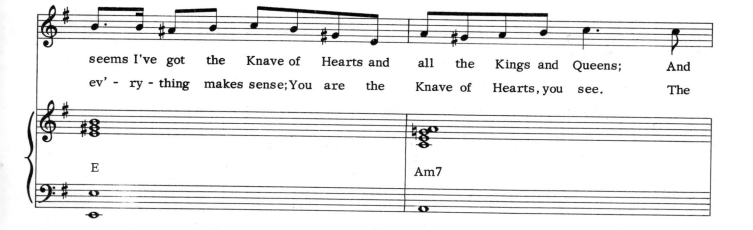

We'll Find Our Day

cue:___

TILDA: You've been dreaming, my girl, if you think that he loves you.

FANNY: I made a great impression on him at dinner.
I don't think he ever met anyone like me before.

TILDA: I should say so.

FANNY: Ah, you're only jealous. I'll show you.   (She moves towards Nicholas)
Nicholas. . . .

(She has changed from the girl we know. All is slow motion and
dream-like.
NICHOLAS turns to FANNY, puts down his book and opens his arms.)

(Set transforms to church. BOYS could enter as choirboys and sing
the harmonies.)

Here I Am (Reprise)

*cue:*_____

NICHOLAS: Stop!!
SQUEERS: (freezes) Who cried stop? (savagely)
NICHOLAS: I did, Squeers. This must not go on.
SQUEERS: Must not go on? (He releases Smike and turns to confront NICHOLAS)
NICHOLAS: I say, must not! And shall not! I will prevent it.

(NICHOLAS pulls SMIKE away from SQUEERS
 and faces Mr and Mrs SQUEERS threatingly.)

(During the song the BOYS run riot and overpower the SQUEERS family.

Books are thrown, desks are upturned and the furniture is wrecked.

MRS SQUEERS is forced to take large doses of Brimstone.

WACKFORD JUNIOR's head is immersed in the Brimstone bowl.

FANNY is surrounded by screaming boys.

Eventually the SQUEERS family is driven out and are chased by some
of the boys.

Crescendo of noise is followed by sudden silence and blackout.)

Don't Let Life Get You Down
and In The Warm Light of A Brand New Day (Reprise)

*cue:*____

BROWN: Do you know, I've got a feeling....

SMEETON: Yes, I know what you mean. I'm sure it must have happened really.

(Starts to hum "Don't let life get you down".)

I can remember. I'm sure that's why I'm so happy.

(He leads the BOYS into the Reprise of "DON'T LET LIFE GET YOU DOWN"

followed by the Reprise of "IN THE WARM LIGHT OF A BRAND NEW DAY")

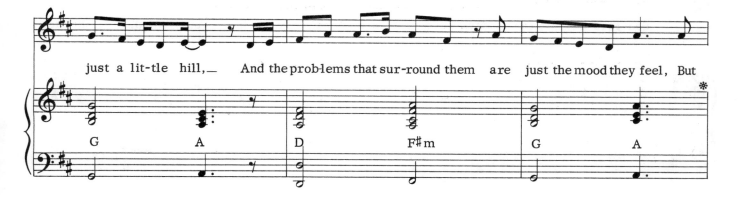

E-ven though the world might let you down. ___

Asus 4   A   D   G   Asus 4   A

Don't let life, ___ don't let life, ___ Don't let life ___ get you down! ___

D   G   D   G   D   G

In The Warm Light Of A Brand New Day

a tempo ♩ = 74

A   C#m   G   D

Esus 4   E   A   C#m   G   D

care _____ In the warm light _____ of a brand_new_

Dma7   F#m/C#   Bm7   E11

day. ____

A   C#m   G   D

Esus 4   E   A   C#m

G   D   Esus 4   E   F#

Believe

*cue:*_____

HEADMASTER: The breaking-up assembly? (He laughs) Well, that might be a good thing.

SMEETON: Could we rehearse every day?

HEADMASTER: Yes.

SMEETON: Instead of the Daily Test?

HEADMASTER: Well.... Yes, all right.

(The class cheer and gather round the HEADMASTER and MISS GRANT talking about the parts they want to play.

Lights fade on everyone except NICHOLLS who enters and walks forwards

Lights fade on everybody except NICHOLLS who enters and walks forwards away from the excited but silent group of BOYS.)

You said that we were in - sin - cere;
Ev' - ry - thing I say I feel;
They've brought the fin - al cur - tain down;

But now our play is done, ____
The world of make - be - liev - - - ing
They've turned the lights down low, ____

EDITOR'S NOTE   CHORUS

And now our life's __ be - gun. ____
We'll leave be - hind __ for real. ____
The peo - ple start __ to go. ____

n.b. see libretto
for allocation of
CHORUS words.   } Be -

lieve,   be - lieve in what I tell you, ___   now the feel-ing's changed. _____ Be-

G   F   C

lieve,   be - lieve in what I'm say-ing ___   how the world's a stage. _____ Be -

ff G   F   C

lieve,   be - lieve in what I   tell   you ___   now the

G   F

feel-ing's changed. _____

C   Am/C   F/C   [timp. roll]   C
                              F/C

CURTAIN
FALLS

Dotheboys Rock (Reprise)

Duration: at Director's discretion.

CHORUS (Tutti)

Do-the- boys rock! yeh yeh!—

Do-the- boys roll! yeh yeh! __ Do-the-boys rock!

yeh yeh! __ Do the boys roll! yeh yeh!—

Do the boys rock, Do __ the boys rock and roll! __

MR SQUEERS

Well, I'm

Do the boys rock! yeh yeh!— Do the boys roll! yeh yeh!—

Do the boys rock! yeh yeh!— Do the boys roll! yeh yeh!—

Do the boys rock, Do— the boys rock and roll!—

Printed in England by WEST CENTRAL PRINTING CO. LTD., London and Suffolk